WHAT I READ

MY BOOK READING JOURNAL

PROPERTY OF

ADDR: _____

ADDR: _____

CITY/STATE/ZIP: _____

EMAIL: _____

FACEBOOK: _____

TWITTER: _____

DISCLAIMER

The opinions expressed in this Journal are mine and do not represent the opinions of anyone else, and any resemblance between these opinions and those of others is purely coincidental and not intentional.

If this Journal is found, please return it to me.

TABLE OF CONTENTS

☆☆☆☆☆ _____ 31

☆☆☆☆☆ _____ 32

☆☆☆☆☆ _____ 33

☆☆☆☆☆ _____ 34

☆☆☆☆☆ _____ 35

☆☆☆☆☆ _____ 36

☆☆☆☆☆ _____ 37

☆☆☆☆☆ _____ 38

☆☆☆☆☆ _____ 39

☆☆☆☆☆ _____ 40

☆☆☆☆☆ _____ 41

☆☆☆☆☆ _____ 42

☆☆☆☆☆ _____ 43

☆☆☆☆☆ _____ 44

☆☆☆☆☆ _____ 45

☆☆☆☆☆ _____ 46

☆☆☆☆☆ _____ 47

☆☆☆☆☆ _____ 48

☆☆☆☆☆ _____ 49

☆☆☆☆☆ _____ 50

☆☆☆☆☆ _____ 51

☆☆☆☆☆ _____ 52

☆☆☆☆☆ _____ 53

☆☆☆☆☆ _____ 54

☆☆☆☆☆ _____ 55

☆☆☆☆☆ _____ 56

☆☆☆☆☆ _____ 57

☆☆☆☆☆ _____ 58

☆☆☆☆☆ _____ 59

☆☆☆☆☆ _____ 60

☆☆☆☆☆ _____ 61

☆☆☆☆☆ _____ 62

☆☆☆☆☆ _____ 63

☆☆☆☆☆ _____ 64

☆☆☆☆☆ _____ 65

☆☆☆☆☆ _____ 66

☆☆☆☆☆ _____ 67

☆☆☆☆☆ _____ 68

☆☆☆☆☆ _____ 69

☆☆☆☆☆ _____ 70

☆☆☆☆☆ _____ 71

☆☆☆☆☆ _____ 72

☆☆☆☆☆ _____ 73

☆☆☆☆☆ _____ 74

☆☆☆☆☆ _____ 75

☆☆☆☆☆ _____ 76

☆☆☆☆☆ _____ 77

☆☆☆☆☆ _____ 78

☆☆☆☆☆ _____ 79

☆☆☆☆☆ _____ 80

☆☆☆☆☆ _____ 81

☆☆☆☆☆ _____ 82

☆☆☆☆☆ _____ 83

☆☆☆☆☆ _____ 84

☆☆☆☆☆ _____ 85

☆☆☆☆☆ _____ 86

☆☆☆☆☆ _____ 87

☆☆☆☆☆ _____ 88

☆☆☆☆☆ _____ 89

☆☆☆☆☆ _____ 90

☆☆☆☆☆ _____ 91

☆☆☆☆☆ _____ 92

☆☆☆☆☆ _____ 93

☆☆☆☆☆ _____ 94

☆☆☆☆☆ _____ 95

☆☆☆☆☆ _____ 96

☆☆☆☆☆ _____ 97

☆☆☆☆☆ _____ 98

☆☆☆☆☆ _____ 99

☆☆☆☆☆ _____ 100

☆☆☆☆☆ _____ 101

☆☆☆☆☆ _____ 102

☆☆☆☆☆ _____ 103

☆☆☆☆☆ _____ 104

☆☆☆☆☆ _____ 105

☆☆☆☆☆ _____ 106

☆☆☆☆☆ _____ 107

☆☆☆☆☆ _____ 108

☆☆☆☆☆

TITLE

AUTHOR

GENRE/SERIES

CHARACTERS

PLOT

MY REACTION/FAVORITE QUOTE/BEST SCENE:

☆☆☆☆☆

TITLE

AUTHOR

GENRE/SERIES

CHARACTERS

PLOT

MY REACTION/FAVORITE QUOTE/BEST SCENE:

☆☆☆☆☆

TITLE

AUTHOR

GENRE/SERIES

CHARACTERS

PLOT

MY REACTION/FAVORITE QUOTE/BEST SCENE:

TITLE

AUTHOR

GENRE/SERIES

CHARACTERS

PLOT

MY REACTION/FAVORITE QUOTE/BEST SCENE:

☆☆☆☆☆

TITLE

AUTHOR

GENRE/SERIES

CHARACTERS

PLOT

MY REACTION/FAVORITE QUOTE/BEST SCENE:

☆☆☆☆☆

TITLE

AUTHOR

GENRE/SERIES

CHARACTERS

PLOT

MY REACTION/FAVORITE QUOTE/BEST SCENE:

☆☆☆☆☆

TITLE

AUTHOR

GENRE/SERIES

CHARACTERS

PLOT

MY REACTION/FAVORITE QUOTE/BEST SCENE:

☆☆☆☆☆

Title _____

Author _____

Genre/Series _____

Characters _____

_____

_____

_____

_____

Plot _____

_____

_____

_____

_____

_____

_____

_____

_____

My Reaction/Favorite Quote/Best Scene: _____

_____

_____

_____

_____

_____

_____

_____

_____

☆☆☆☆☆

TITLE

AUTHOR

GENRE/SERIES

CHARACTERS

PLOT

MY REACTION/FAVORITE QUOTE/BEST SCENE:

☆☆☆☆☆

TITLE

AUTHOR

GENRE/SERIES

CHARACTERS

PLOT

MY REACTION/FAVORITE QUOTE/BEST SCENE:

☆☆☆☆☆

TITLE

AUTHOR

GENRE/SERIES

CHARACTERS

PLOT

MY REACTION/FAVORITE QUOTE/BEST SCENE:

TITLE

AUTHOR

GENRE/SERIES

CHARACTERS

PLOT

MY REACTION/FAVORITE QUOTE/BEST SCENE:

☆☆☆☆☆

TITLE

AUTHOR

GENRE/SERIES

CHARACTERS

PLOT

MY REACTION/FAVORITE QUOTE/BEST SCENE:

☆☆☆☆☆

TITLE

AUTHOR

GENRE/SERIES

CHARACTERS

PLOT

MY REACTION/FAVORITE QUOTE/BEST SCENE:

☆☆☆☆☆

TITLE

AUTHOR

GENRE/SERIES

CHARACTERS

PLOT

MY REACTION/FAVORITE QUOTE/BEST SCENE:

☆☆☆☆☆

TITLE

AUTHOR

GENRE/SERIES

CHARACTERS

PLOT

MY REACTION/FAVORITE QUOTE/BEST SCENE:

☆☆☆☆☆

TITLE

AUTHOR

GENRE/SERIES

CHARACTERS

PLOT

MY REACTION/FAVORITE QUOTE/BEST SCENE:

☆☆☆☆☆

TITLE

AUTHOR

GENRE/SERIES

CHARACTERS

PLOT

MY REACTION/FAVORITE QUOTE/BEST SCENE:

☆☆☆☆☆

TITLE

AUTHOR

GENRE/SERIES

CHARACTERS

PLOT

MY REACTION/FAVORITE QUOTE/BEST SCENE:

☆☆☆☆☆

TITLE

AUTHOR

GENRE/SERIES

CHARACTERS

PLOT

MY REACTION/FAVORITE QUOTE/BEST SCENE:

☆☆☆☆☆

TITLE

AUTHOR

GENRE/SERIES

CHARACTERS

PLOT

MY REACTION/FAVORITE QUOTE/BEST SCENE:

☆☆☆☆☆

TITLE

AUTHOR

GENRE/SERIES

CHARACTERS

PLOT

MY REACTION/FAVORITE QUOTE/BEST SCENE:

☆☆☆☆☆

TITLE

AUTHOR

GENRE/SERIES

CHARACTERS

PLOT

MY REACTION/FAVORITE QUOTE/BEST SCENE:

☆☆☆☆☆

TITLE

AUTHOR

GENRE/SERIES

CHARACTERS

PLOT

MY REACTION/FAVORITE QUOTE/BEST SCENE:

☆☆☆☆☆

TITLE

AUTHOR

GENRE/SERIES

CHARACTERS

PLOT

MY REACTION/FAVORITE QUOTE/BEST SCENE:

☆☆☆☆☆

TITLE

AUTHOR

GENRE/SERIES

CHARACTERS

PLOT

MY REACTION/FAVORITE QUOTE/BEST SCENE:

☆☆☆☆☆

TITLE

AUTHOR

GENRE/SERIES

CHARACTERS

PLOT

MY REACTION/FAVORITE QUOTE/BEST SCENE:

☆☆☆☆☆

TITLE

AUTHOR

GENRE/SERIES

CHARACTERS

PLOT

MY REACTION/FAVORITE QUOTE/BEST SCENE:

☆☆☆☆☆

TITLE

AUTHOR

GENRE/SERIES

CHARACTERS

PLOT

MY REACTION/FAVORITE QUOTE/BEST SCENE:

☆☆☆☆☆

TITLE

AUTHOR

GENRE/SERIES

CHARACTERS

PLOT

MY REACTION/FAVORITE QUOTE/BEST SCENE:

☆☆☆☆☆

TITLE

AUTHOR

GENRE/SERIES

CHARACTERS

PLOT

MY REACTION/FAVORITE QUOTE/BEST SCENE:

☆☆☆☆☆

TITLE

AUTHOR

GENRE/SERIES

CHARACTERS

PLOT

MY REACTION/FAVORITE QUOTE/BEST SCENE:

☆☆☆☆☆

TITLE

AUTHOR

GENRE/SERIES

CHARACTERS

PLOT

MY REACTION/FAVORITE QUOTE/BEST SCENE:

☆☆☆☆☆

TITLE

AUTHOR

GENRE/SERIES

CHARACTERS

PLOT

MY REACTION/FAVORITE QUOTE/BEST SCENE:

☆☆☆☆☆

TITLE

AUTHOR

GENRE/SERIES

CHARACTERS

PLOT

MY REACTION/FAVORITE QUOTE/BEST SCENE:

☆☆☆☆☆

TITLE

AUTHOR

GENRE/SERIES

CHARACTERS

PLOT

MY REACTION/FAVORITE QUOTE/BEST SCENE:

☆☆☆☆☆

TITLE

AUTHOR

GENRE/SERIES

CHARACTERS

PLOT

MY REACTION/FAVORITE QUOTE/BEST SCENE:

☆☆☆☆☆

TITLE

AUTHOR

GENRE/SERIES

CHARACTERS

PLOT

MY REACTION/FAVORITE QUOTE/BEST SCENE:

☆☆☆☆☆

TITLE

AUTHOR

GENRE/SERIES

CHARACTERS

PLOT

MY REACTION/FAVORITE QUOTE/BEST SCENE:

☆☆☆☆☆

TITLE

AUTHOR

GENRE/SERIES

CHARACTERS

PLOT

MY REACTION/FAVORITE QUOTE/BEST SCENE:

☆☆☆☆☆

TITLE

AUTHOR

GENRE/SERIES

CHARACTERS

PLOT

MY REACTION/FAVORITE QUOTE/BEST SCENE:

☆☆☆☆☆

TITLE

AUTHOR

GENRE/SERIES

CHARACTERS

PLOT

MY REACTION/FAVORITE QUOTE/BEST SCENE:

☆☆☆☆☆

TITLE

AUTHOR

GENRE/SERIES

CHARACTERS

PLOT

MY REACTION/FAVORITE QUOTE/BEST SCENE:

☆☆☆☆☆

TITLE

AUTHOR

GENRE/SERIES

CHARACTERS

PLOT

MY REACTION/FAVORITE QUOTE/BEST SCENE:

☆☆☆☆☆

TITLE

AUTHOR

GENRE/SERIES

CHARACTERS

PLOT

MY REACTION/FAVORITE QUOTE/BEST SCENE:

☆☆☆☆☆

TITLE

AUTHOR

GENRE/SERIES

CHARACTERS

PLOT

MY REACTION/FAVORITE QUOTE/BEST SCENE:

☆☆☆☆☆

TITLE

AUTHOR

GENRE/SERIES

CHARACTERS

PLOT

MY REACTION/FAVORITE QUOTE/BEST SCENE:

☆☆☆☆☆

TITLE

AUTHOR

GENRE/SERIES

CHARACTERS

PLOT

MY REACTION/FAVORITE QUOTE/BEST SCENE:

☆☆☆☆☆

TITLE

AUTHOR

GENRE/SERIES

CHARACTERS

PLOT

MY REACTION/FAVORITE QUOTE/BEST SCENE:

☆☆☆☆☆

TITLE

AUTHOR

GENRE/SERIES

CHARACTERS

PLOT

MY REACTION/FAVORITE QUOTE/BEST SCENE:

☆☆☆☆☆

TITLE

AUTHOR

GENRE/SERIES

CHARACTERS

PLOT

MY REACTION/FAVORITE QUOTE/BEST SCENE:

☆☆☆☆☆

TITLE

AUTHOR

GENRE/SERIES

CHARACTERS

PLOT

MY REACTION/FAVORITE QUOTE/BEST SCENE:

☆☆☆☆☆

Title _____

Author _____

Genre/Series _____

Characters _____

_____

_____

_____

_____

Plot _____

_____

_____

_____

_____

_____

_____

_____

_____

My Reaction/Favorite Quote/Best Scene: _____

_____

_____

_____

_____

_____

_____

_____

☆☆☆☆☆

TITLE

AUTHOR

GENRE/SERIES

CHARACTERS

PLOT

MY REACTION/FAVORITE QUOTE/BEST SCENE:

☆☆☆☆☆

TITLE

AUTHOR

GENRE/SERIES

CHARACTERS

PLOT

MY REACTION/FAVORITE QUOTE/BEST SCENE:

☆☆☆☆☆

TITLE

AUTHOR

GENRE/SERIES

CHARACTERS

PLOT

MY REACTION/FAVORITE QUOTE/BEST SCENE:

☆☆☆☆☆

TITLE

AUTHOR

GENRE/SERIES

CHARACTERS

PLOT

MY REACTION/FAVORITE QUOTE/BEST SCENE:

☆☆☆☆☆

TITLE

AUTHOR

GENRE/SERIES

CHARACTERS

PLOT

MY REACTION/FAVORITE QUOTE/BEST SCENE:

☆☆☆☆☆

TITLE

AUTHOR

GENRE/SERIES

CHARACTERS

PLOT

MY REACTION/FAVORITE QUOTE/BEST SCENE:

☆☆☆☆☆

TITLE

AUTHOR

GENRE/SERIES

CHARACTERS

PLOT

MY REACTION/FAVORITE QUOTE/BEST SCENE:

☆☆☆☆☆

TITLE

AUTHOR

GENRE/SERIES

CHARACTERS

PLOT

MY REACTION/FAVORITE QUOTE/BEST SCENE:

☆☆☆☆☆

TITLE

AUTHOR

GENRE/SERIES

CHARACTERS

PLOT

MY REACTION/FAVORITE QUOTE/BEST SCENE:

☆☆☆☆☆

TITLE

AUTHOR

GENRE/SERIES

CHARACTERS

PLOT

MY REACTION/FAVORITE QUOTE/BEST SCENE:

☆☆☆☆☆

TITLE

AUTHOR

GENRE/SERIES

CHARACTERS

PLOT

MY REACTION/FAVORITE QUOTE/BEST SCENE:

☆☆☆☆☆

TITLE

AUTHOR

GENRE/SERIES

CHARACTERS

PLOT

MY REACTION/FAVORITE QUOTE/BEST SCENE:

☆☆☆☆☆

TITLE

AUTHOR

GENRE/SERIES

CHARACTERS

PLOT

MY REACTION/FAVORITE QUOTE/BEST SCENE:

☆☆☆☆☆

TITLE

AUTHOR

GENRE/SERIES

CHARACTERS

PLOT

MY REACTION/FAVORITE QUOTE/BEST SCENE:

☆☆☆☆☆

TITLE

AUTHOR

GENRE/SERIES

CHARACTERS

PLOT

MY REACTION/FAVORITE QUOTE/BEST SCENE:

☆☆☆☆☆

TITLE

AUTHOR

GENRE/SERIES

CHARACTERS

PLOT

MY REACTION/FAVORITE QUOTE/BEST SCENE:

☆☆☆☆☆

TITLE

AUTHOR

GENRE/SERIES

CHARACTERS

PLOT

MY REACTION/FAVORITE QUOTE/BEST SCENE:

☆☆☆☆☆

TITLE _____

AUTHOR _____

GENRE/SERIES _____

CHARACTERS _____

_____

_____

_____

_____

PLOT _____

_____

_____

_____

_____

_____

_____

_____

_____

MY REACTION/FAVORITE QUOTE/BEST SCENE: _____

_____

_____

_____

_____

_____

_____

_____

_____

☆☆☆☆☆

TITLE

AUTHOR

GENRE/SERIES

CHARACTERS

PLOT

MY REACTION/FAVORITE QUOTE/BEST SCENE:

☆☆☆☆☆

TITLE _____

AUTHOR _____

GENRE/SERIES _____

CHARACTERS _____

_____

_____

_____

_____

PLOT _____

_____

_____

_____

_____

_____

_____

_____

_____

MY REACTION/FAVORITE QUOTE/BEST SCENE: _____

_____

_____

_____

_____

_____

_____

_____

☆☆☆☆☆

TITLE

AUTHOR

GENRE/SERIES

CHARACTERS

PLOT

MY REACTION/FAVORITE QUOTE/BEST SCENE:

☆☆☆☆☆

TITLE

AUTHOR

GENRE/SERIES

CHARACTERS

PLOT

MY REACTION/FAVORITE QUOTE/BEST SCENE:

☆☆☆☆☆

TITLE

AUTHOR

GENRE/SERIES

CHARACTERS

PLOT

MY REACTION/FAVORITE QUOTE/BEST SCENE:

☆☆☆☆☆

TITLE

AUTHOR

GENRE/SERIES

CHARACTERS

PLOT

MY REACTION/FAVORITE QUOTE/BEST SCENE:

☆☆☆☆☆

TITLE

AUTHOR

GENRE/SERIES

CHARACTERS

PLOT

MY REACTION/FAVORITE QUOTE/BEST SCENE:

☆☆☆☆☆

TITLE

AUTHOR

GENRE/SERIES

CHARACTERS

PLOT

MY REACTION/FAVORITE QUOTE/BEST SCENE:

☆☆☆☆☆

TITLE

AUTHOR

GENRE/SERIES

CHARACTERS

PLOT

MY REACTION/FAVORITE QUOTE/BEST SCENE:

☆☆☆☆☆

TITLE ....

AUTHOR ....

GENRE/SERIES ....

CHARACTERS ....

....

....

....

....

PLOT ....

....

....

....

....

....

....

....

MY REACTION/FAVORITE QUOTE/BEST SCENE: ....

....

....

....

....

....

....

....

....

☆☆☆☆☆

TITLE

AUTHOR

GENRE/SERIES

CHARACTERS

PLOT

MY REACTION/FAVORITE QUOTE/BEST SCENE:

☆☆☆☆☆

TITLE

AUTHOR

GENRE/SERIES

CHARACTERS

PLOT

MY REACTION/FAVORITE QUOTE/BEST SCENE:

☆☆☆☆☆

TITLE

AUTHOR

GENRE/SERIES

CHARACTERS

PLOT

MY REACTION/FAVORITE QUOTE/BEST SCENE:

☆☆☆☆☆

TITLE

AUTHOR

GENRE/SERIES

CHARACTERS

PLOT

MY REACTION/FAVORITE QUOTE/BEST SCENE:

☆☆☆☆☆

TITLE

AUTHOR

GENRE/SERIES

CHARACTERS

PLOT

MY REACTION/FAVORITE QUOTE/BEST SCENE:

☆☆☆☆☆

TITLE

AUTHOR

GENRE/SERIES

CHARACTERS

PLOT

MY REACTION/FAVORITE QUOTE/BEST SCENE:

☆☆☆☆☆

TITLE

AUTHOR

GENRE/SERIES

CHARACTERS

PLOT

MY REACTION/FAVORITE QUOTE/BEST SCENE:

☆☆☆☆☆

TITLE

AUTHOR

GENRE/SERIES

CHARACTERS

PLOT

MY REACTION/FAVORITE QUOTE/BEST SCENE:

☆☆☆☆☆

TITLE ....

AUTHOR ....

GENRE/SERIES ....

CHARACTERS ....

....

....

....

....

PLOT ....

....

....

....

....

....

....

....

....

MY REACTION/FAVORITE QUOTE/BEST SCENE: ....

....

....

....

....

....

....

....

....

☆☆☆☆☆

TITLE

AUTHOR

GENRE/SERIES

CHARACTERS

PLOT

MY REACTION/FAVORITE QUOTE/BEST SCENE:

☆☆☆☆☆

TITLE

AUTHOR

GENRE/SERIES

CHARACTERS

PLOT

MY REACTION/FAVORITE QUOTE/BEST SCENE:

☆☆☆☆☆

TITLE

AUTHOR

GENRE/SERIES

CHARACTERS

PLOT

MY REACTION/FAVORITE QUOTE/BEST SCENE:

☆☆☆☆☆

TITLE

AUTHOR

GENRE/SERIES

CHARACTERS

PLOT

MY REACTION/FAVORITE QUOTE/BEST SCENE:

☆☆☆☆☆

TITLE

AUTHOR

GENRE/SERIES

CHARACTERS

PLOT

MY REACTION/FAVORITE QUOTE/BEST SCENE:

☆☆☆☆☆

TITLE

AUTHOR

GENRE/SERIES

CHARACTERS

PLOT

MY REACTION/FAVORITE QUOTE/BEST SCENE:

☆☆☆☆☆

TITLE

AUTHOR

GENRE/SERIES

CHARACTERS

PLOT

MY REACTION/FAVORITE QUOTE/BEST SCENE:

☆☆☆☆☆

TITLE

AUTHOR

GENRE/SERIES

CHARACTERS

PLOT

MY REACTION/FAVORITE QUOTE/BEST SCENE:

☆☆☆☆☆

TITLE

AUTHOR

GENRE/SERIES

CHARACTERS

PLOT

MY REACTION/FAVORITE QUOTE/BEST SCENE:

☆☆☆☆☆

TITLE

AUTHOR

GENRE/SERIES

CHARACTERS

PLOT

MY REACTION/FAVORITE QUOTE/BEST SCENE:

☆☆☆☆☆

TITLE

AUTHOR

GENRE/SERIES

CHARACTERS

PLOT

MY REACTION/FAVORITE QUOTE/BEST SCENE:

☆☆☆☆☆

TITLE

AUTHOR

GENRE/SERIES

CHARACTERS

PLOT

MY REACTION/FAVORITE QUOTE/BEST SCENE:

☆☆☆☆☆

TITLE

AUTHOR

GENRE/SERIES

CHARACTERS

PLOT

MY REACTION/FAVORITE QUOTE/BEST SCENE:

☆☆☆☆☆

TITLE

AUTHOR

GENRE/SERIES

CHARACTERS

PLOT

MY REACTION/FAVORITE QUOTE/BEST SCENE:

☆☆☆☆☆

TITLE

AUTHOR

GENRE/SERIES

CHARACTERS

PLOT

MY REACTION/FAVORITE QUOTE/BEST SCENE:

☆☆☆☆☆

TITLE

AUTHOR

GENRE/SERIES

CHARACTERS

PLOT

MY REACTION/FAVORITE QUOTE/BEST SCENE:

☆☆☆☆☆

TITLE

AUTHOR

GENRE/SERIES

CHARACTERS

PLOT

MY REACTION/FAVORITE QUOTE/BEST SCENE:

☆☆☆☆☆

TITLE

AUTHOR

GENRE/SERIES

CHARACTERS

PLOT

MY REACTION/FAVORITE QUOTE/BEST SCENE:

☆ ☆ ☆ ☆ ☆

TITLE

AUTHOR

GENRE/SERIES

CHARACTERS

PLOT

MY REACTION/FAVORITE QUOTE/BEST SCENE:

☆☆☆☆☆

TITLE

AUTHOR

GENRE/SERIES

CHARACTERS

PLOT

MY REACTION/FAVORITE QUOTE/BEST SCENE:

☆☆☆☆☆

TITLE _____

AUTHOR _____

GENRE/SERIES _____

CHARACTERS _____

_____

_____

_____

PLOT _____

_____

_____

_____

_____

_____

_____

_____

MY REACTION/FAVORITE QUOTE/BEST SCENE: _____

_____

_____

_____

_____

_____

_____

_____

☆☆☆☆☆

TITLE

AUTHOR

GENRE/SERIES

CHARACTERS

PLOT

MY REACTION/FAVORITE QUOTE/BEST SCENE:

☆☆☆☆☆

TITLE

AUTHOR

GENRE/SERIES

CHARACTERS

PLOT

MY REACTION/FAVORITE QUOTE/BEST SCENE:

☆☆☆☆☆

TITLE

AUTHOR

GENRE/SERIES

CHARACTERS

PLOT

MY REACTION/FAVORITE QUOTE/BEST SCENE:

☆☆☆☆☆

TITLE

AUTHOR

GENRE/SERIES

CHARACTERS

PLOT

MY REACTION/FAVORITE QUOTE/BEST SCENE:

☆☆☆☆☆

TITLE

AUTHOR

GENRE/SERIES

CHARACTERS

PLOT

MY REACTION/FAVORITE QUOTE/BEST SCENE:

☆☆☆☆☆

TITLE

AUTHOR

GENRE/SERIES

CHARACTERS

PLOT

MY REACTION/FAVORITE QUOTE/BEST SCENE:

☆☆☆☆☆

TITLE

AUTHOR

GENRE/SERIES

CHARACTERS

PLOT

MY REACTION/FAVORITE QUOTE/BEST SCENE:

☆☆☆☆☆

TITLE

AUTHOR

GENRE/SERIES

CHARACTERS

PLOT

MY REACTION/FAVORITE QUOTE/BEST SCENE:

☆☆☆☆☆

TITLE

AUTHOR

GENRE/SERIES

CHARACTERS

PLOT

MY REACTION/FAVORITE QUOTE/BEST SCENE:

☆☆☆☆☆

TITLE

AUTHOR

GENRE/SERIES

CHARACTERS

PLOT

MY REACTION/FAVORITE QUOTE/BEST SCENE:

CPSIA information can be obtained at www.ICGtesting.com
Printed in the USA
BVOW08s1910100315

391110BV00011B/312/P